The Story Tree

Terry Deary

Illustrated by
Rhian Nest James

GINN

Chapter 1

Sabulana sat in the tree and giggled. It was a big tree, a strong tree, maybe the biggest in the whole jungle. "The boys will never find me here," she laughed, and hugged a huge branch.

Then she heard their voices. "She came this way," Uzo said. He was angry.

Sabulana looked down on his thick, bushy
hair and his thick, fat arms.

"She came this way," Meshack agreed.
His hair was as thin as rainwater and his
arms were as thin as twigs.

"When I get my hands on that Sabulana
I'll beat her!" Uzo cried.

"I'll beat her too!" Meshack promised.

"She must be hiding," Uzo growled and
looked around. He didn't look above his
head where Sabulana crouched.

3

"If you ask me, I think she must be hiding," Meshack said.

"I didn't ask you," Uzo snapped. "Just look hard."

Meshack's head turned left, then right. Somewhere in the forest some monkeys chattered. Uzo's bushy hair swung from side to side. The Subulana did a very silly thing. She pulled a large nut from the tree and held it over Uzo's head.

"I'll beat her till she cries!" the fat boy hissed.

Sabulana let go of the nut. It tumbled through the air and landed with a smack on Uzo's head.

"Ahooh!" the boy yelped. Still he would not have looked up – but Sabulana let out a snorting laugh.

Uzo's narrow brown eyes peered up into the branches. His lips curled back in a furious snarl.

"Come down here, girl," he ordered.

"Yes, come down here," Meshack echoed.

"Why?" Sabulana asked, wide-eyed and pretending not to know.

"Come down and I'll beat you," Uzo promised.

"Hah! Then I'd be stupid to come down, wouldn't I?" she replied cheekily.

Uzo's eyes narrowed till they vanished in folds of flesh. "I order you to come down," he said.

"He *orders* you," Meshack said. "And he's the son of the Oba."

Sabulana sniffed. "I wouldn't come down for the son of Onyankopon the god of the Ashanti. So I'm certainly not coming down for the son of the village chief."

Meshack's mouth fell open but he could think of nothing to say. Uzo spoke. "If the girl won't come down, then we'll have to go up. Meshack!"

"I'm too small to reach," Meshack squeaked.

Uzo sighed. "Then bend over while I stand on you back," the chief's son ordered.

Meshack did as he was told and Uzo began to reach for the first low branch. Sabulana backed away towards the trunk of the tree. The branches were so thick they made a platform over the forest floor. Uzo's grinning head broke through the leaves. His dark face shone with sweat.

The girl reached backwards and grabbed at something soft and heavy... a vine! Keeping her eyes on the Oba's ugly son she tugged it from the tree and swung it over her head.

The smile slid from the boy's face like rain from a leaf. "What's wrong, Uzo? Scared? Scared of a girl?"

He shook his head dumbly. "Nnnng!" he managed to grunt. At last he made his fear-frozen lips work. "No – but I'm scared of a snake!" he wailed, and fell from the tree on to his little friend.

Sabulana looked at the "vine" in her hand. The vine looked back at her with two unblinking eyes. It wriggled. It ran a purple, forked tongue over its bloodless lips. It looked hungry and Sabulana looked like its next meal.

The girl dropped the snake. It fell through the branches. There was a squawk from under the tree and a crashing. The snake had landed on the bullying boys. They ran back to the village quick as the whisk of a crocodile's tail.

Sabulana staggered back along the branch, feeling a little faint. Suddenly there was no branch there to step on. She fell through the carpet of leaves. Down she tumbled and twisted. Down into a darkness as deep as the village well.

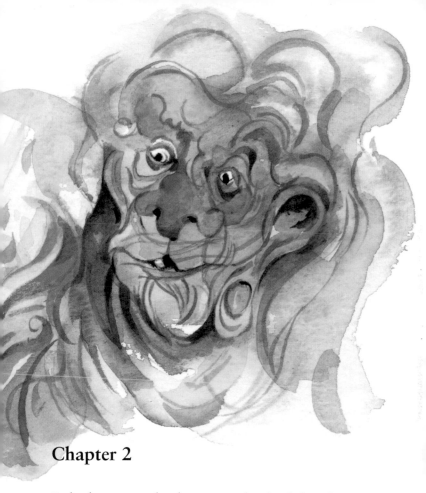

Chapter 2

Sabulana crashed on to a bed of dried leaves and lay still. She wasn't hurt, just a little shocked.

She blinked and looked around her. It was dark down here. The only light spilled through the hole in the roof that Sabulana had just made. She didn't seem to be under the tree – she knew that she was *inside* the tree.

Sabulana groaned and sat up. The leaves crackled. It seemed a long way up to the roof.

The trunk of the tree was every shade of brown, and wrinkled like an old woman's face. Two pieces of black glass glittered in the folds like an old woman's eyes. A small piece of ivory sat there like the single tooth of an old woman's smile.

Sabulana jumped and cried out suddenly. She found she really was looking into the face of a very old woman. It seemed to be carved into the tree... until the mouth opened and the wrinkled face spoke.

"A nice mess you've made of my roof!"

"S-s-sorry," Sabulana managed to say.

"Next time, use the door," the old woman snapped.

"Yes... yes, I will." Sabulana stared at the wall of branches. A curtain of leaves seemed to hang over a gap in the wall. She guessed that was the door.

"So, welcome to Araba's home. What brings you here, child?"

Sabulana licked her lips. "Er... I was running away from some boys. From Meshack and Uzo... Uzo's the son of the village Oba. They want to beat me!"

"Hmm," Araba mumbled. "And what have you done to deserve that?"

"Nothing!" Sabulana cried. She twisted the edge of her white cotton dress miserably and sniffed. "Our teacher, Miss Gowon, gave us a test," she said.

"And a bright, sharp girl like you would do well in a test?" the old woman asked.

Sabulana looked up sharply. "What's wrong with that?"

The black-glass eyes sparkled. "Quite a temper, young Sabulana, quite a temper! That won't help!"

Sabulana glared at the shadows where the old woman sat. "It isn't fair! I beat all the boys in the test. I beat everyone. I'm the cleverest in the class. Probably the cleverest in the village. What's wrong with that?"

The glass eyes glittered. "You are a girl, Sabulana. Girls fetch wood and girls fetch water. Girls help their mothers in the fields and girls help their mothers in the house."

Sabulana jumped to her feet. She ran to the door and pushed her way through the leaf curtain. She almost ran straight into the back of two men.

"Uzo said she climbed this tree and threw a snake at him!" one of the men said. Sabulana knew the voice at once. It was her father.

She was just about to cry out when the other man said, "You will have to take her from the school. Make her work in the fields till she is old enough to marry!"

Sabulana crept back into the shadow of the door, afraid, and listened.

Her father grumbled, "A wilful girl like that? Who will pay good money to marry a girl like that? No, she needs beating every day for a year until she learns to keep that sharp tongue inside her mouth."

The girl tested her tongue with the tip of her finger. "It isn't sharp at all!" she murmured.

"It's growing dark," her father said. "She'll come home when she's hungry," and the men vanished into the darkening air.

Sabulana went back inside the tree. Old Araba was silent in her shadows. "It isn't fair. Boys don't have to do all those things. Boys have an easy life!"

"Boys have a hard life," the old woman told her. "Boys have to be best at everything. And the son of the Oba has to be best of all. To be second best in a test is a disgrace for Uzo. But to be beaten by a girl is the greatest shame in the world."

"It isn't fair," the girl said again. "How can I show them how stupid they all are?" Araba didn't answer the question. She simply said, "Sit down, Sabulana. I'll tell you an old, old story... "

Chapter 3

"Long, long ago, in a village not so very far from here, there lived an old, old couple. And the old, old couple were so poor and small and thin that people called them the skinny couple.

As time went by the village people found that thieves were taking food and money from their huts when they were working in the fields. Then one day a man was ill – too ill to go out to the fields. As he lay in his sick-bed he saw two scrawny little thieves creep in and steal his bag of cowrie shells – all the money he'd saved.

He staggered from his bed and cried out, "Thieves! The skinny couple are the thieves!"

The workers ran back from the fields. "Did you see them?"

"Yes, I did! My shells! They took my lovely cowrie shells!"

"Now, have no fear, we'll get them back... and all the other stolen things." The workers marched down to the hut – the shabby little hut owned by the skinny couple.

"Let us in!" the angry village people cried, "We mean to search your hut."

"To search our hut! You can't do that," the skinny little woman moaned. "We didn't do it. Go away, it wasn't us. We never saw a single cowrie shell, so go away."

"Then let us search," the Oba's wife said. "If your hut is empty then we'll go away. But if we find a single shell we'll beat you thieving pair with whips and drive you from this village."

"Then search," the old man sighed. The workers searched. They searched some more, and then they searched and searched again. And, after searching for an hour, they hadn't found a single thing.

"We know you have the money here!" the Oba's wife said. "Tell us where it is or else we'll go and fetch our whips."

"Then fetch your whips," the skinny man shrugged.

When the villagers had gone to fetch their whips he reached up to the roof and took the box of cowrie shells down. The skinny couple had hidden it in the thatch.

"Now run!" the skinny woman cried, and trotted down the forest path.

"Look! There they go!" the Oba's wife called. "Catch them... beat them... flog them... whip them!"

"Quick! Climb up that tree," the skinny woman urged her husband. So they climbed the nearest tree, there on the forest edge.

"Come down!" the village people cried.

"We won't!" the skinny couple screamed.

"Then we'll stay here until you do," the Oba's wife said, and she sat there on the ground.

The skinny man said, in a whisper, "When they go back to eat their suppers then we'll run away."

The village people didn't go. They stayed all night and all next day, they stayed for weeks and then for months. At last they moved their huts and stayed forever by the tree.

The skinny couple ate the tree's fruit, then its leaves, and then they started on the bark. Then strange things began to happen.

They became as thin as spiders and their teeth as sharp as knives. When the cold came they grew thick coats of shabby fur. Hanging from the tree their hands and feet grew hard as any wood. Then, one day, they woke to find that each had grown a tail. They shrieked and chattered at each other and they swung from branch to branch.

And, to this day, the people of the trees are skinny men and skinny women. Hairy creatures with long tails, chattering nonsense to each other. Now and then they watch the humans and they try to copy them. And, of course, they have kept their thieving ways.

That's right, the skinny couple turned into monkeys."

Chapter 4

Sabulana was angry.

She pushed through the curtain of leaves and left Araba in her tree home. "What a stupid woman!" she muttered. "Here I am, in danger of a beating. If Uzo and Meshack don't get me then my father will. And all Araba does is tell me some old story!"

Sabulana walked to the forest edge. Behind her, in the shadows of the trees, something large gave a deep growl. Parrots squawked in panic and clattered into the air. She shuddered. "I suppose that story meant I should go and live up a tree," she snorted. "Well, I'm not going to be a snake's supper or a baboon's breakfast, thank you!"

She hurried over the empty fields towards the huts of the village where the smell of cooking yams made her mouth water. "And I'm not eating leaves," she added.

A thin moon was rising and washing the clearing in a watery light. The workers had all gone home and the cooking fires gave the village a warm, safe glow.

Sabulana stopped. She looked up at the moon and she blinked. She smiled. "*That's* what the story meant! The moon can change from fat to thin and back again. The skinny couple could change. So *I* can change!"

She marched towards the huts, happier now. She didn't see four eyes in the

22

shadows following her. "That's what Araba was trying to tell me – maybe she isn't so stupid after all. I can't change the *world*, but I *can* change *myself!*" she said.

Two shadows slid from the shelter of the Oba's hut and stood in the path. "We knew you'd have to come this way," Uzo said nastily, waving a large stick under Sabulana's nose.

"We knew," Meshack said.

Sabulana smiled at the boys. "I understand," she grinned.

"Eh?" Uzo blinked.

"What?" Meshack gasped.

The girl walked past the surprised boys and towards her hut. The boys scurried after her. "I understand how hard it is to be a boy," she was saying.

"Is it?"

"It is?"

"Yes. You don't have to beat me now. I won't try to make you look silly in class again," she promised. "I'm going to change from this night on."

"That's all right then," skinny Meshack nodded.

"No it's not!" Uzo roared at his weedy friend. "I'm the chief's son! Everyone will laugh at me if I don't give her at least one good slap with this stick."

Meshack raised the stick in the air. He lowered it slowly.

Sabulana was nowhere to be seen.

"She ran away," Meshack said.

"Why didn't you stop her?" the chief's son cried. "We'll have to get her on the way to school tomorrow," he muttered.

The large creature at the edge of the forest roared again. The boys looked towards the sound. "Let's get the goats in the pen," Uzo said quickly.

As the boys hurried into the village Sabulana was bursting into her mother's hut. Her mother looked up from grinding

the maize. "Your father has been looking for you," she said.

"I know," the girl said miserably. "Everybody wants to beat me. I suppose you want to beat me because I'm late."

Her mother shrugged. "You are too late to fetch the water, it's true. But I won't beat you. You can just go to bed thirsty."

25

Sabulana hung her head. "Father will beat me," she groaned. "He thinks I threw a snake at Uzo. I didn't!"

"Then tell your father that you didn't."

"But I *did!*" Sabulana groaned. "It just fell on him. No one will believe me. I can't see any way out."

The woman dusted maize flour from her hands and smiled. "There is always a way out. And talking about snakes reminds me of the story of Anansi and the snake..."

And she told her daughter the old story.

Chapter 5

"Long, long ago, in a village not so very far from here, lived the famous Anansi.

Now sometimes Anansi appeared as a spider and sometimes Anansi appeared as a man. Whatever he was, he was a great, great cheat. And he always wanted to make himself look clever and important.

Now, only the Oba in the village used to get important letters in the post. Some days the postman called and left the letters... some days the postman called to say there were no letters. No other person in the village had the postman call. It made the Oba very grand.

Anansi was jealous. Anansi had to have his own postman. And so he went to see the snake.

"I want you, Snake, to call at my hut every morning."

"Yes-s, Anans-si."

"I need a postman who will call each morning."

"Yes-s, Anans-si, I'll do that."

"Even when I have no mail, I want you please to call," the boastful spider said.

"Oh, yes-s, Anans-si, I'll do that. Now how much will you pay?" the snake asked, and it licked its pale, hard lips.

"I'll pay you anything you want," Anansi promised. He, of course, would make quite sure he didn't have to pay.

The snake's great fangs flashed in the light, a glittering, greedy smile. "Each day I call I'll take a bite – I'll take a bite out of your head!"

28

Anansi thought this was a tiny price to pay to be the most important in the village. The snake had just a tiny mouth. It wouldn't take too much.

The next day dawned, the village watched and saw the snake call at Anansi's house. "Good morning, s-sir, no pos-st today."

"Ah, thank-you, postman, call again!" Anansi cried so all the people heard.

"And, now, I'll take a bite out of your head," the snake hissed happily.

"A tiny bite," Anansi trembled, and he held his head down.

But the snake had such a mouth he bit off half Anansi's head! He licked his bloodless lips and hissed, "Until tomorrow, then!"

"Oh, dear," Anansi thought, "I can't take any more of that. I'll have to make a cunning plan."

He thought and thought, and thought and thought, and then he thought again. At last he smiled and left the hut to visit his old friend the rabbit.

"Ah, Brother Rabbit! My best friend. I must invite you to my house. Come round for supper, stay the night!" Anansi said.

The rabbit came.

Anansi fed him very well, then made a bed out in the hall. "Now, you sleep here," he said. "There's just one thing... my cousin Snake is calling round at first light in the morning. Now, if he calls when I'm asleep, let him in at the door!" Anansi went to bed and laughed himself to sleep, thinking himself *so* clever.

The rabbit couldn't sleep. He knew his friend was always up to tricks. So Rabbit dug and dug and dug, and then he dug some more. He dug a hole beneath the wall and ran off to his home.

When morning came the snake arrived. He rattled on the door. Anansi gasped to see the hole beneath the wall and Rabbit gone.

Still the snake knocked on the door and rattled to come in.

Anansi ran round to the back to try to run away. The snake had blocked the back door with a stone. The snake knocked on the door and called, "I'll break it down if you don't let me in!"

Anansi groaned, Anansi moaned. At last he grabbed the cooking pot and jammed it on his head. So when the snake broke down the door and went to bite Anansi's head the snake broke both his fangs!

And so Anansi lost a friend – and Snake lost his front teeth. At least the sly Anansi kept his head, just when it seemed that all was lost."

Chapter 6

Sabulana lay awake in bed that night. She puzzled over her mother's story and wondered how it could help her.

She fell asleep, then wakened when she heard the rattle of rain against the tin roof of the hut. She looked up at the roof and smiled. Her father kept tin patches for the roof under his own hut. She nodded. They would be her protection, like Anansi's cooking pot.

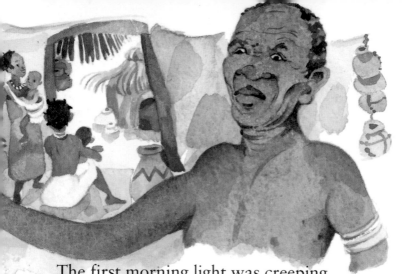

The first morning light was creeping through the door. The girls and women in the hut were stirring. Sabulana joined them in the morning chores; collecting wood for fires and water for cooking. She bathed in the river before slipping back into her white school dress and carrying the water back to the family hut.

As she stirred the yam porridge her father came into the hut. "Aha! There you are, girl. I want to have a word with you."

"Yes, Father," Sabulana mumbled, and scooped out a bowl of porridge for him.

"You have upset the Oba's son. And if the Oba's son is upset then the Oba will be upset. And if the Oba is upset he will want someone punished. Well, he's not going to punish me!"

"No, Father."

"So I'll go to see him this morning. See what he wants doing. But it will probably be a beating... and I'll have to take you away from school."

Tears pricked Sabulana's eyes at the thought of leaving the school. They ran down the side of her nose and dropped into the porridge. She stirred them in angrily.

"Come to my hut after school this afternoon," the man said.

"Yes, Father."

Sabulana fed the children, then washed the dishes before she crept out of the hut and round to her father's hut. After searching it for five minutes she slid out with a grim smile on her face, and two tin patches in her hand.

She dusted off her white dress and looked round to see that no one was watching. Carefully she hid the tin shapes inside her dress and set off down the path to the school at the end of the village.

At the bottom step of the school stood a crowd of boys talking excitedly. As they saw Sabulana they went silent and parted to make a way for the girl. But that way was blocked by Uzo and Meshack.

"You made me look foolish yesterday," the chief's son said in a loud voice – loud enough for all the silent boys to hear.

"I know. I said I was sorry and that it won't happen again," Sabulana said gently.

Uzo looked uneasy. "It's a matter of honour," he said.

"Ah, well," she shrugged. "In that case, maybe Meshack would like to hit me

here," she said, pointing just above her belt.

The skinny boy looked around. The boys were waiting. He had to do something. He rushed forward and jabbed a punch at the girl.

There was a muffled *clang!* A shocked pause. A scream. "I think I've broken my hand!" Meshack wailed and ran off clutching his fist.

Uzo moved behind Sabulana and let fly with his stick across her back. There was

the same *clang!* Then a *crack!* as the stick
snapped in two. Then a cry of rage from
the chief's son as Sabulana ran up the
steps into the classroom.

Miss Gowon was quietly marking books.
She looked up and smiled at Sabulana.

"Just what is going on outside,
Sabulana?"

Sabulana sat at her desk and sighed.
"Uzo says I made him look foolish in the
test. He and Meshack want to beat me.
I've tried to say sorry, twice. What more
can I do?"

"You can keep trying. Like the woman in
the story of the stepson and the black-
maned lion..."

And Miss Gowon told the girl the old
story.

Chapter 7

"Long, long ago, in a village not so very far from here, there lived a woman with her husband and his son.

But when the husband died she was left with just the stepson. She was a kindly woman. Although the child was not her own she loved him like a mother. She gave him shelter, gave him warmth and gave him every favourite food to make him happy. Yet the boy was never happy.

He never let the woman hug him and he never let her tell him stories. He never let her kiss him and, worst of all, he never, never smiled for her.

She asked her friends what she could do. They didn't know the answer.

At last she went and saw the wise man of the village and told him her sad tale.

The wise man nodded in the way that wise men always do. He thought a while and then he said, "I think I have the answer. What you need is some strong spell to bind the boy to you. And for the spell you need some hair you've taken from a lion."

The woman smiled; she knew the Oba had tame lions. Perhaps he'd give her the hair she needed. The wise man shook his head, the way that wise men do. "The hair must be from a wild lion... one with a mane as black as ebony."

The woman trembled and the woman shook. She didn't dare to look at those wild lions... let alone go near one... let alone take hair from one! She went home very sad.

The stepson was as cold as ever; never smiling, never speaking, eating just a scrap of food before he went off to his bed. And so the woman made her mind up.

That was it – she had to go. She took a slice of goat meat and she crept down to the river. There the lion's cave was waiting with its mouth as dark and fearsome as the black-maned lion itself. That night she dropped the meat and ran.

Next morning, when she went for water, no meat lay outside the cave. That night she dropped another piece of meat, and this time hid behind a tree to see what would happen. The lion crept out from the cave and sniffed the meat before he swallowed it in one huge gulp.

The woman almost fainted as she staggered to her hut. But next night, as the sun set, she returned and placed another slice of meat outside the cave.

This time, when the lion came, she stood beside the tree. The lion stared at her with golden eyes, but swallowed up the meat and licked its lips.

The fourth night she grew bolder, and dropped the meat but stood quite near.

The fifth night she held out the meat and let it drop just as the lion raised its fearsome head. At last she held out the meat and let the lion take it from her hand.

The lion grew to trust her, and she grew
to trust the beast. She stroked its mane, it
licked her hand.

After twenty nights, or maybe more, she
took a sharp knife from her belt. As the
lion chewed a bone she sliced a piece of
mane and tucked it in her belt.

She hurried, joyful, to the wise man. "Look!" she cried. "I have it here! The hair of the black-maned lion. Now you'll make the spell for me?"

"The spell? What spell?" the wise man murmured, and he laughed as wise men do. "You know the spell. Treat your stepson like the lion. Careful, gentle, till he trusts you. Time will weave the spell for you."

So the woman went home happy. Her courage, love and patience won the boy's heart just as it had with the lion.

Soon he took his food and started smiling at her stories. Still, the story he loved best was... yes, the one about the black-maned lion!"

Chapter 8

Sabulana nodded. "I'll keep trying," she promised.

But all that day, something troubled her. She waited till the other pupils had all gone home. When the teacher was alone Sabulana went to her desk. "Miss Gowon, my father says he'll take me away from this school."

The teacher frowned. "Oh, no, that would be too sad, Sabulana. You are the brightest girl I have ever taught. This school should be just a start for someone like you. You could go on to college in the city. The village would be proud of you.

Perhaps I should have a word with your father."

"No! No!" Sabulana said quickly. "My father wants a word with me this evening anyway. I'll ask him then."

But the truth was she didn't know what she was going to say to her father. He wasn't in his hut. "He'll see you after supper," her mother told her when they went to the river to wash clothes.

Sabulana climbed the river bank and looked across the fields. The tallest tree in all the forest pushed its head up to the evening sky. And the girl remembered Araba – the old woman who lived in the tree.

Sabulana wanted to tell the woman she was sorry for rushing out the night before. Tell her how helpful the story was... and ask for more help now.

She crossed the fields and found the patch that led into the forest. Two shapes, a fat one and a thin one, stood astride the path. "Hello, Uzo," she smiled. "Am I forgiven yet?" (Patience, time and care, she remembered from the story of the black-maned lion.)

To her surprise, Uzo smiled. He looked quite pleasant when he smiled. "Of course," he said. "Come here."

He stretched a hand towards her but he didn't move. "We knew you'd come this way again!" his thin friend squeaked. And Meshack's eyes were popping out on stalks. He hopped from foot to foot in excitement.

Sabulana didn't understand what was wrong. She stopped. "No," Uzo said. "Another step!"

She took another step. She stepped on to a leafy carpet – and the carpet vanished under her feet. Sabulana screamed in fear as she fell into the deep black hole. The boys screamed with delight. Their grinning faces appeared at the rim of the hole and grinned down at the dazed girl.

"I thought you said that you'd forgiven me," she groaned.

"For the test – but not for that trick with the tin in your dress this morning," Uzo said. "See if your tin can save you from this!" he growled as he dropped a snake into the hole with her.

Sabulana wanted to scream and scramble from the trap. But that was what the boys were waiting for. Instead she closed her eyes and thought. She thought about the black-maned lion. An animal would not attack unless she tried to attack it first. (Patience, time and care, she thought.)

The boys stared at her, wide-eyed and wondering at her calm as the snake curled up on the floor of the trap.

Sabulana used all her clever mind to work it out. The boys wouldn't have caught a poisonous snake – too dangerous. And they wouldn't have put a poisonous snake in the pit with her. Even the Oba's son couldn't get away with murder. No, she decided. It was a harmless snake.

The girl looked up. "All right, Uzo, I think we're even now." She held up a hand.

The fat boy took it and helped her out. He looked at her with new respect. He gave a brief nod. "You are brave," he said. "We are even," he said quietly and turned to run back to the village.

Sabulana dusted her dress and headed for the leafy curtain in the giant tree. In the shadows the old face watched her.

"Araba," the girl said. "I have a problem. My father."

"Let me tell you an old, old story..." the woman began.

Chapter 9

"Long, long ago, in a village not so very far from here, there lived a caterpillar.

One day the caterpillar decided to visit the house of his friend the hare. But it took him *such* a long time to crawl there. By the time he arrived the hare had gone out. Still, he slipped inside the hare's home to wait for his return.

The hare came back. He saw the tracks outside his house and called out, frightened, "Who's there? Who's that there inside my house?"

The caterpillar liked to have a joke. He took a deep breath and roared out in his loudest voice, "I am here. I am Shango, god of War. I can grind the rhinoceros into the earth, I can crush the elephant into dust. I am unbeatable!"

The hare was terrified. "I can't fight Shango, god of War! A little thing like me!

He'll blow me away like a summer cloud. I'm off!" he cried, and scuttered down the road.

There he ran – whap! slap! bam! – into the leopard. "What's wrong, Hare?" the leopard asked. "You look like you've had a scare, Hare," said the leopard (who liked a joke as much as the caterpillar.)

But, when the hare had told his story, the leopard laughed. "I'll deal with this rascal for you. I'm afraid of no one," the leopard said, and set off for the hare's house.

"Who dares to scare my friend the hare?" the leopard roared.

The caterpillar took a deep breath and roared out in his loudest voice, "I am here. I am Shango, god of War. I can grind the rhinoceros into the earth, I can crush the elephant into dust. I am unbeatable!"

The leopard had never been so scared in his life. "Of course I *would* tear the villain to pieces," he whispered to the hare, "but I have a bit of a headache just at the moment. Perhaps we should tell the rhinoceros what this fellow's been saying about her."

When they told her, the rhinoceros was furious. "The cheek!" she cried. "We'll see who'll grind who into the dust!" and she trotted up the path until it shook.

"Who's there in Hare's lair, daring to scare without a care?"

The caterpillar took a deep breath and roared out in his loudest voice, "I am here. I am Shango, god of War. I can grind the rhinoceros into the earth, I can crush the elephant into dust. I am unbeatable!"

"In that case," said the shivering rhino," I think you'd better have a word with my friend the elephant."

But even the elephant came away with a trembling trunk. The animals stood and quivered and quaked and quarrelled about what to do... until along came the frog.

"Leave this to me!" the crafty animal said. At he door he called, "Who's there in Hare's lair?

The caterpillar took a deep breath and roared out in his loudest voice, "I am here. I am Shango, god of War. I can grind the rhinoceros into the earth, I can crush the elephant into dust. I am unbeatable!"

"Ah!" the frog called back, "Well, let me tell you, Shango, I am the great jumper who can jump twenty times my own

height. And if I land on you I'll break you like a twig."

There was a silence. Then the caterpillar's tiny voice called out, "To tell the truth I'm not Shango. In fact I'm not really all that big. In fact... to tell the truth, I'm Hare's friend Caterpillar! Please don't jump on me, Mr Jumper."

"Come out now, if you dare, or I shall come and drag you out!" the frog croaked. And when the animals saw the cringing caterpillar crawl out they didn't know whether to laugh... or feel ashamed. They laughed."

Chapter 10

Sabulana laughed as she hurried back across the evening fields. She knew now how to deal with her father.

The new moon hung low in the purple sky and the laughing girl cried to it, "I am unbeatable!" She nodded to the moon, "It's true! If you really believe something then other people will believe it too. You just stay there and watch what happens when I visit my father!"

Sabulana hurried into the family hut to change from her dusty school clothes into her best red cotton dress. She ran a comb through her hair until it hung neatly, then fastened a ribbon into it. Her mother smiled, "Good luck, Sabulana."

She grinned back. "Don't worry. I am unbeatable!"

She hurried across to her father's hut and pushed the wicker door open. He sat in

the light of a lantern sharing a pipe with
the friend who was going to help with the
beating. "Good evening, Father,"
Sabulana said with a bright smile.

The smile confused the men. "Ah – um!
Yes. I wanted a word with you, girl."

"Oh, I *know*, Father. And I've been
longing to have a word with you."

The pipe almost dropped from the man's
drooping mouth. "You have?"

"About school," Sabulana went on
eagerly. "Miss Gowon says I'm the best
pupil she has ever had."

"She does?" her father said.

"Oh, yes. I told her that I get my brains
from my father, of course," Sabulana
shrugged.

"Naturally," her father smiled. "Did you
hear that, Hassan?" he said to his friend.
"The best pupil in the school – gets her
brains from her father."

"It doesn't show," Hassan said sourly.
"Yesterday you said the girl was too clever
for her own good."

"Ah, yes. That was yesterday," Sabulana's father smiled. "But imagine what a prize such a clever girl will be in four or five years' time. Some lucky man will pay me a fortune to marry her. Can you cook, girl?"

"Yes, Father, but..."

"And do you work as hard as your mother in the hut?"

"Yes, Father, but..."

"Then you are worth ten cows at least in marriage payment!" her father chuckled and rubbed his hands.

Sabulana's smile had faded now. "But, father, Miss Gowon says that I should go to college in the city!"

The men raised their eyebrows. "Why?" Hassan asked.

"I thought I may become a teacher, like Miss Gowon," Sabulana said. She stopped. She hadn't known that was what she wanted until she said it.

"How long will that take?" her father asked.

"Two – three years. I don't know," the girl replied.

Her father sucked on his pipe. "No, no! Not for a girl worth twenty cows in marriage," he sighed.

"*If* anyone will marry her," Hassan put in nastily.

"What do you mean?" Sabulana's father asked sharply.

"I mean *if* anyone wants to marry a girl who waves her cleverness in front of your face like an elephant waves its trunk. Don't forget how she upset poor little Uzo, the Oba's son!" Hassan reminded his friend.

Sabulana's father nodded sadly. "True."

"Remember, the Oba wishes to see the girl. By the time he's finished with her she may not be worth a dead goat, never mind ten cows!" Hassan went on.

The sad father shook his head. "That is true, Hassan, my friend." He turned his sad eyes on his daughter. "Get yourself across to the Oba's hut at once," he ordered, and turned to fill his pipe.

Sabulana ducked out of the hut. She looked across to the Oba's huge hut. Sounds of laughter and dancing came from the doorway. She wasn't ready yet to face the Oba.

She ran across the fields to the moon-shadowed forest. She stumbled through the bushes and stepped carefully round Uzo's trap. There was no light in Araba's tree home. But she knew the old woman was there, waiting in the dark.

"I will tell you an old, old story..." Araba began.

Chapter 11

"Long, long ago, in a village not so very far from here, there lived a rich man who had many cattle and two wives.

Each wife had a daughter. The daughter of the chief wife was called Katsina. She was pretty – but very proud and very lazy.

The daughter of the second wife, N'Gozi, was not so pretty – but she was thoughtful and hard-working. One day they were out gathering firewood and they found they had strayed too far from home. Night was falling and leopards waited in the trees to pounce on careless travellers.

"There's a cottage there," N'Gozi said. "Perhaps the old woman at the door can give us shelter for the night."

"I hope the hut is clean," Katsina sneered. "I'm used to nothing but the best!"

"Of course," the ancient woman smiled.
"You're both welcome to spend the night.
Just step inside – we'll bar the door.
You're safe as safe as safe in here."

"I hope you have some food, I'm
starved," Katsina said.

"That's if it is no trouble," gentle N'Gozi
said.

"Of course, of course!" The woman
smiled a toothless smile and turned to her
small oven. She served the girls two bowls
of food and placed them on the table. One
bowl was filled with all the very finest
food – the other bowl had scraps of stale
old food.

Proud Katsina took the bowl with all the
fine, rich food. N'Gozi took the scraps
and whispered, "What a kind old
woman."

"I hope you have some place to sleep,"
Katsina said. "I'm used to nothing but the
best."

"That's if it is no trouble," kind N'Gozi
added.

63

"I have two beds," the woman said, and
showed them to another room. One bed
was soft and filled with straw, with rich
blankets warm enough for any chilling
right. The other bed was one thin, flat rug
on the ground.

Katsina took the fine, fat bed while poor
N'Gozi took the rug. At least we're safe
from hungry beasts," the kind girl said.

Next morning, when the sun had driven
all the wild beasts to their lairs, the good
N'Gozi rose. She rolled her blanket, swept
the floor and helped the woman gather
wood. Katsina stayed in bed until the
breakfast food was served.

Again the food was good and bad –
again Katsina took the good. Then
N'Gozi washed the bowls and tidied up
the hut.

Before they left the woman said, "I have
two gifts." She placed two bowls upon the
table. Both were covered with a cloth and
tied up very tight.

"I hope the present is a good one,"
proud Katsina said. "I'm used to nothing
but the best."

"You're very kind," the quiet N'Gozi added.

"There's just one thing!" the woman warned. "You must not open up the bowls until you reach your home."

Both girls promised. Then they waved goodbye and headed down the path to home.

Katsina soon grew tired. "Let's stop and open up the gifts," she said.

"We promised that we wouldn't," her kind sister warned.

"Huh!" the proud Katsina grunted, then she stomped off to their home. When she reached her hut she tore the covering off the bowl. "I hope it's just what I deserve!" she smiled.

It was. For soon she screamed. Something foul and yellow drifted out and smothered cruel Katsina's face. There it clung; it made her look the ugliest creature in the world.

N'Gozi's bowl was filled with every type of jewel, in bracelets, anklets and gold necklaces. There was also a tiny hut that grew and grew until it was a full-size home.

Proud Katsina with her ugly yellow face never found a husband. She was punished for her cruel ways.

But men from every village round about came to see N'Gozi and ask her if she'd marry them. Good N'Gozi had the choice of any man she wanted. So, of course, she chose the best. Fair reward for her hard work."

Chapter 12

Sabulana stayed another hour and listened to Araba's tales. "Yes, I understand," she said at last. "I'm like N'Gozi in the story of the two sisters. If I work hard then everyone will want me. I can choose my future for myself."

"You can, my child," Araba agreed. "And freedom to choose is true freedom."

"But I'll never go to college while my father wants me married off," Sabulana moaned.

"And does your father have the last say in your village?" Araba asked.

The girl smiled in the wood-scented darkness and softly said, "No. He doesn't, does he?" She jumped to her feet. She knew what she had to do. "I'll see you tomorrow, Araba," Sabulana promised.

"Perhaps," the faint voice answered.

Sabulana hurried over the fields, through

the village and up the steps to the Oba's hut. As she entered, the music and the dancing stopped. A hundred faces in the crowded hall turned to stare at her.

The Oba sat on a high wooden chair at the end of the long room. Sabulana raised her chin and marched down the corridor of people. The Oba had a face as wrinkled as Araba's tree and eyes as fierce as any eagle.

"And you must be Sabulana," he said. "The girl I have to beat." His voice was deeper than a leopard's growl.

"Yes, sir," the girl replied.

"I hear that you have been upsetting my son," he rumbled.

Sabulana licked her lips. "Yes, Oba," she said.

The man leaned forward. All the hall was hushed. Suddenly a yellow-toothed smile split his wooden face. "Well done!" he chuckled.

As he laughed the villagers breathed again and gently laughed too. The Oba's chief wife chuckled till the tears ran down her face. Sabulana looked confused.

The chief explained. "If Uzo wants to be a man he has to learn to face a challenge. He's always had things far too easy. His mother spoils him," the Oba said.

The woman wiped her tears and poked her husband with a sharp finger. "His father spoils him too," she said. The chief wife turned back to the girl. "Does your father spoil you?" she asked.

"Not really," Sabulana admitted.

"But he must be very proud of you," the Oba chuckled.

Sabulana saw her chance and said quickly, "Not as proud as he could be." The villagers grew silent once again.

"Explain," the Oba said.

"I'd like to leave the village when I'm old enough. I want to go to the city. I want to go to the college and learn to be a teacher."

There was a gasp from the villagers but the Oba simply nodded. "No one has ever left this village to become a teacher," he said. "The honour for your father would be great; the honour for our village would be great."

Sabulana took a deep breath. "So, may I go, Oba?"

The old man's eyes narrowed. "Tests in school are not everything. You beat my son Uzo – perhaps my son is not so clever as he thinks!"

"He isn't!" the chief wife laughed.

"So can you show me what will make little Sabulana a teacher?" the Oba demanded.

The girl smiled. "You are setting me a task."

"I am," the Oba said. He was puzzled. "So?"

"It reminds me of an old, old story," Sabulana said.

The Oba leaned forward eagerly. "So, you know old stories, do you, girl?"

She nodded.

"Then that shall be your task," the chief said. He waved a hand to all the villagers who were gathered in the hall. "Enough of singing and dancing tonight!" he roared. "We will have a story!"

Sabulana looked at all the faces as they turned towards her. "I am unbeatable," she told herself. The villagers sat on the floor of the hall. The Oba stood and waved her into his seat before he joined his people on the floor.

Sabulana took a deep breath and began.

Chapter 13

"Long, long ago, in a village not so very far from here, there lived a very selfish man. He lived with his daughter, Abiola. And she looked after him because his wife was dead.

Abiola looked after him so well he made his mind up she would never marry and leave him.

Now the girl was pretty, and many men would happily have made her their wife. The selfish man drove every one of them away. Abiola's friends all married, but she was left alone. She begged her father to let her marry.

"No."

She pleaded with her father.

"No."

She asked and asked and asked and asked, until the selfish man could say "No!" no more.

So he said "Yes... BUT..."

"But?" Abiola asked.

"But any man who wants to marry you must carry out three tasks," the selfish man said.

"What three tasks?" she asked.

"First, he must take his shirt off and sit in a room full of mosquitoes without moving or driving the insects off. Second, he must eat some powdered pepper without making a sound or pulling a face. Lastly he must tell a story that lasts from sunrise to sunset!"

Abiola knew that no one could perform these tasks. Young men came from many miles, for young Abiola was very lovely. Many tried... and each one failed, of course.

But one young farmer lived quite near and he was rich and clever. He'd also loved the girl for many years. He made his plans, then asked if he could try his luck.

First the selfish man shut the young man in a room full of mosquitoes. Then he sat down to watch him. At first the young farmer sat quite still, but then the insects started to bite.

The farmer then began to tell a story. "I saw a cow at market just last week," he said. "It was the most peculiar cow. It was purple here," he said, and slapped his shoulder. "It was green here," he went on, and slapped his chest. "The cow had an orange nose," he said, slapping his nose, "and it was yellow on the foreleg," he explained, slapping his elbow.

The trick was that he was killing the insects as he slapped his body. The foolish selfish man was too busy listening to the story to notice. And so the farmer passed test one.

Then the farmer went outside and slyly scattered corn around his feet. He placed the red-hot pepper in his mouth. At that moment hens came out and started pecking at the corn. "Shoo!" he cried, "These hens are such a plague. Shoo! Shoo! Shoo!"

The trick was that as the man said "Shoo!" he was blowing out hot pepper. The foolish selfish man was too busy chasing hens to notice. And so the farmer passed the second test.

And then, at sunrise the next day, the village gathered round to hear the tale that had to last from dawn till dusk. The farmer looked at all the people, and then began, "I saw a mouse steal corn from sacks inside my barn one day. It picked up a grain of corn and it took it to its nest, then it picked up another grain of corn and took it to its nest, then it picked up another grain of corn..." and on and on the story went with every grain of corn the mouse took out.

The village people went away. Only the selfish man stayed behind until the sun set, and even he had trouble trying to stay awake. "Then the barn was empty!" the farmer finished as the sun went down.

"And I think I've won your daughter."

So he had. And since he was a handsome man, as well as rich and clever, Abiola was more than happy.

You don't need me to tell you that they lived for many, many happy years."

Chapter 14

Sabulana finished the story. The villagers looked at the Oba. The Oba looked at the girl. "Wonderful!" he said.

"Ohh!" the villagers gasped. "Wonderful," they agreed. Most people agreed with the Oba.

"Tomorrow we start to build a new village council hut," the Oba said. "We have a ceremony when we raise the new ridge pole. We have dances. We having singing. Now we can have a story. Sabulana is out new village story-teller!" the old man said.

The village people cheered. The girl was slapped and patted on the head until her head was sore.

She didn't get to bed till after moon-set. So, at sunrise, she was tired, but she helped her mother with the water and the cooking before she hurried to the story tree. She rushed to tell Araba all the news. But the story tree seemed strangely lifeless in the morning light. "Araba?" Sabulana called.

There was no reply. She pushed the leaf curtain aside and let the morning light spill through the gap. The hollow tree was empty. There was no old woman there. Sabulana wondered if there ever had been.

The wooden wall where Araba had sat was just a twisted trunk. Perhaps the odd shape could have been mistaken for an old woman. Those two black stones were where her eyes had been – that piece of ivory looked just like Araba's single tooth.

Sabulana shivered and backed out of the hollow tree. Araba was the story tree and the story tree was Araba. That was all she knew. She stroked the trunk and whispered, "Thank you, Araba. I know I'll get to college in the city, thanks to you. And your stories will go on. I won't let the villagers forget."

Suddenly a voice said, "Talking to a tree! Whatever next?"

Sabulana swung round. A group of twenty men with axes gathered at the edge of the forest. "Hello, young story-teller," one grinned. "Saying goodbye to the old tree, are you?"

"Why would I want to say goodbye?" she asked.

"Because you're cuddling the ridge pole for the new council hut," the man explained.

"You're cutting down this tree?" Sabulana gasped.

"That's right. It's just the size we need."

"You'll kill her!" Sabulana said.

"It's been dead for years, young story-teller," the man said gently.

"But its always been here," she argued.

"As long as I can remember," the man agreed. "But everything dies in the end. Even I remember the old stories from my school days. *You* must remember, story-teller. How God did not mean anything to die."

"I remember," Sabulana said softly. "He sent a message down to earth to say that there would be no death. The messenger was a dog. And the hare heard the message and overtook the dog and brought it down first."

"That's right," the man agreed. "But the hare had heard the message wrong. He told the people that there *was* this thing called Death. And so Death came and it has lived here ever since."

"But not for old Araba," Sabulana argued. "She isn't ready yet to join the great Olorun up in heaven."

"The tree is dead – look, it is hollow

inside," the man said with a tired shake of the head.

"No! She's not dead yet," Sabulana cried. "Look!" She pointed up towards the sky. "Her leaves are green. There's still some life left in her somewhere."

Suddenly the girl stretched up her arms, jumped and clung to the lowest branch. Like the skinny couple she clambered up into the tree. "If you murder this tree then you'll murder me too!" she cried.

The men threw down their axes and sat down on the forest floor. "The Oba wouldn't like that," one man laughed. "But you can't spare a tree just because it's been there as long as our tribe can remember. You can't hang on to the past just for the sake of it!"

And Sabulana remembered the tree's last story.

"You can... you must. Just let me tell you an old, old story..."

Chapter 15

"Long, long ago, in a village not so very far from here, there lived a people called the Machakeni.

  They were a rich people and a happy people. Every year they planted yams and sugar cane and sweet potatoes and bananas. Every year they had a rich, good harvest.

Until, one year, the rains forgot to fall.
The land grew parched and even wild
elephants trampled through their fields.
The Machakeni folk went hungry. They
searched for newer land but always
seemed to be pursued by bad luck.
They took to hunting – chasing animals
through the forests and across the bush
lands.

   Once a group of strong young hunters
chased an antelope into a part of the
forest they had never seen before. A part
where yams and sweet potatoes, sugar
cane and bananas grew as thick and good
as they had done in the rich days.

They brought the tribe there to the new-found garden. "Our misery is over!" they all cried. But strange things happened.

First they felt an evil spirit try to drive them out. Those tribe folk brave enough to face the spirit reached the fruits... but found them fastened to the ground and trees. The fruit could not be picked.

Then still worse luck fell on the tribe. The women went into the forest where they found a hive of bees. A brave girl put her hand into the hive to take the honey out. But, when she tried to take her hand out, it snapped off at the wrist!

The other girls were hungry. One by one they tried to take the honey – one by one their rights hands snapped off at the wrist. Only the Oba's daughter, a clever girl called Sabulana, kept her head. She left the hive alone – so she also kept her hand. She helped the girls to tie their sticks and lift the bundles on their heads. The sad girls went back to the village.

Sabulana told the people that they must throw divining bones – that was the only way that they could get in touch with all the tribe who'd died in ages past.

The wise man of the tribe threw the bones and read the message from the wise old dead. The message said Sabulana must go to the grove of the sacred trees and leave a gift for the forgotten dead of the tribe. And she must go alone.

The tribe went to the edge of the sacred trees and watched as brave Sabulana went into the heart of the forest alone. There she laid a gift for all the forgotten dead.

She told the dead of all the troubles that the tribe had seen. The dead took pity on the living tribe. They gave the girl as much food as she could carry and more. She took it to the edge of the sacred trees where the tribe carried it away.

And then the forgotten dead told brave Sabulana why the tribe had been so cursed. It was because, in all the years of richness, they had never once given thanks to all the guarding spirits of the tribe. The spirits of the dead were angry. That is why they sent the curse.

The girl then swore that they would not forget again. The spirits of the past forgave. They gave an extra gift to all the Machakeni... they gave the lost right hands back to the girls who'd lost them in the bee hives.

And every year the tribe folk sent their gifts in memory of the dead. And every year the crops of yams and sweet potatoes, bananas and sugar cane grew richly in their fields.

The Machakeni never forgot the brave Sabulana – and they never forgot the debt they owed the past. For without the past there is no present."

Chapter 16

Sabulana finished her story and looked down at the men.

They looked in silence at the tree. "The story-teller has a point," one man said slowly. "That tree is older and much wiser than any of us here."

Some others nodded. "The Oba's waiting for the ridge pole," someone pointed out.

"Yes, but that tree over there is almost as tall," the first man said. "And it isn't rotten inside."

More workers joined in with, "That's right," and "True," and "He has a point." Someone said, "So why don't we leave the story-teller's tree and cut the other one down?"

"Yes!" the cry went up. And they marched off with their axes.

Sabulana leaned against the story tree and closed her eyes. She felt old stories flooding through her mind. Funny stories, tragic stories and stories that simply explained why things are as they are.

Her eyes were closed. Still she felt she was being watched. She looked around. Uzo was sitting at the edge of the forest, watching her. The girl went to grab the branch and climb back up the tree.

"No," the Oba's son said quickly. "I don't want to beat you, Sabulana."

"Ah," she nodded but kept a careful eye on the boy.

"I heard your story about the tribe who remembered the spirits of their dead," he said.

"Ah," Sabulana said again.

"You believe in that, do you?"

"What?"

"In remembering the old ways... the old stories... the old trees... the old customs?" he asked. He couldn't seem to look her in the eye. He was strangely shy.

"Yes," the girl said. "I believe in keeping to the old ways."

Uzo nodded. "There is a very old custom in our village, my father says."

"Ah."

"The Oba takes the finest woman in the village to be his chief wife. My father says that, when I am Oba, I should take you for my wife."

"Ah."

The boy looked up. Now it was Sabulana who couldn't meet his eye.

"Miss Gowon says that girls should have freedom these days. Freedom to choose their own husbands."

"But you said you don't like the modern ways," Uzo reminded her, and his eyes turned crafty. "If you like the old ways, you'll stay in the village and be my wife. Forget about the city and the college."

Sabulana clutched the tree and felt the story power flowing through her fingers.

"What I meant to say was... we need to keep the best of the old ways. We can mix them with the best of the new. I want to take my old stories to the city. I want to bring new stories back to the village."

"I see," Uzo said, though he didn't. Sabulana gave a sudden grin. "Oh, cheer up, Uzo."

He just nodded dumbly.

She clicked her fingers. "I know what you need to cheer you up!"

"What?"

She left the comfort of the tree and walked toward Uzo. "You need a story! A funny and exciting story."

"Do you know one?" he asked, brighter.

"Do *I* know a story?" Sabulana laughed. She sat down on the ground beneath the ancient tree and gave a sign for Uzo to sit beside her. When he was seated with his chin resting on his hands she began.

"Long, long ago, in a village not so very far from here, there was a boy called Uzo, the brave and handsome son of the Oba..."